JOY AN IRISH CHRISTMAS

KEITH & KRISTYN GETTY

1. O Children Come
2. O Come Redeemer of the Earth
3. Wonder
4. A Mother's Prayer
5. Silent Night
6. Thou Who Wast Rich Beyond All Splendor
7. Deck the Halls
8. Bethlehem Night
9. For To Us
10. O Hear the Bells
11. Noel, Noel
12. Jesus Tender Shepherd
13. Glorious Light
14. Jesus, Your Name
15. Joy to the World (with Charlotte's Giggles and Miss Eliza's Reel)
16. Go Tell It on the Mountain (with Arkansas Traveler and Toss the Feathers)

Bonus Reels and Jigs include:

Christmas Eve Reel, The Silver Spire Reel, Wassailing Jig,
Bethlehem Traveler's Reel, The Voice and Chime, Crossing the Briney,
and Christmas Ceili

getty music

O Children, Come!

Words and Music by
Kristyn Getty

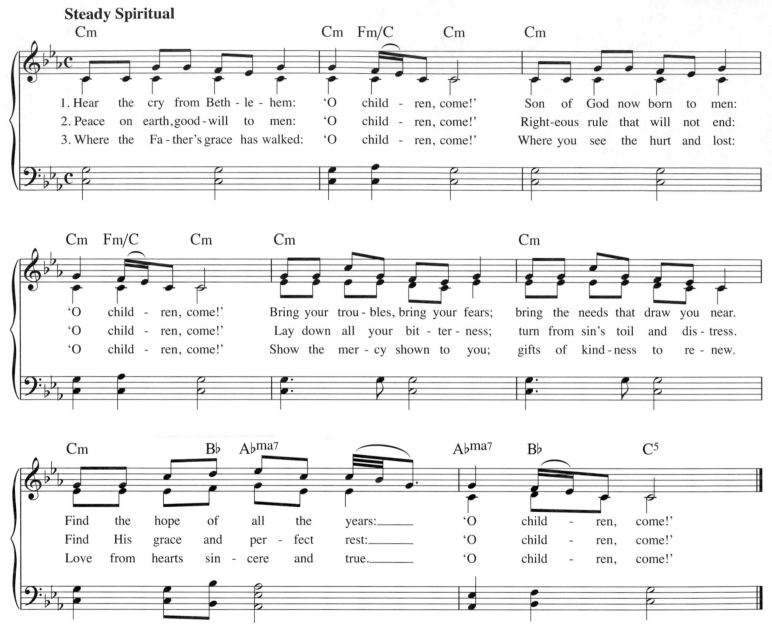

1. Hear the cry from Beth-le-hem: 'O child-ren, come!' Son of God now born to men:
2. Peace on earth, good-will to men: 'O child-ren, come!' Right-eous rule that will not end:
3. Where the Fa-ther's grace has walked: 'O child-ren, come!' Where you see the hurt and lost:

'O child-ren, come!' Bring your trou-bles, bring your fears; bring the needs that draw you near.
'O child-ren, come!' Lay down all your bit-ter-ness; turn from sin's toil and dis-tress.
'O child-ren, come!' Show the mer-cy shown to you; gifts of kind-ness to re-new.

Find the hope of all the years:___ 'O child-ren, come!'
Find His grace and per-fect rest:___ 'O child-ren, come!'
Love from hearts sin-cere and true.___ 'O child-ren, come!'

O Come, Redeemer of the Earth

Music by Keith Getty
Original Lyrics: Ambrose of Milan (397),
translated by John M. Neale (1862)
Lyrics adapted by Kristyn Getty

Wonder

Words and Music by
Keith Getty and Kristyn Getty
Arranged by Keith Getty

Prayerful, Freely

1. I've seen days melt in-to nights___ in cir-cles___ of lights; I've watched a spi-der spin a star be-tween the win-dow box flowers. I've heard you laugh and cry in a sin - gle sigh and a sto-ry___ form___ with-in.

Refrain

Don't let me___ lose my won-der,___ don't let me___ lose

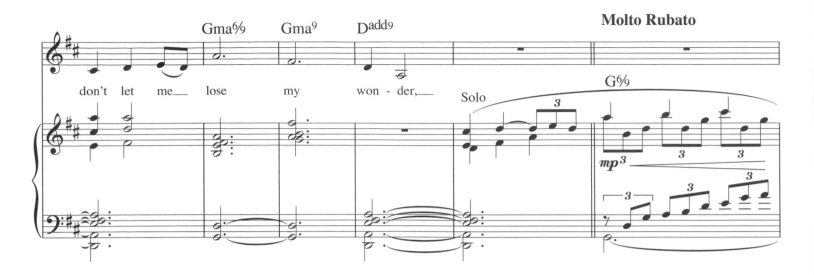

don't let me___ lose my won - der,___ Solo

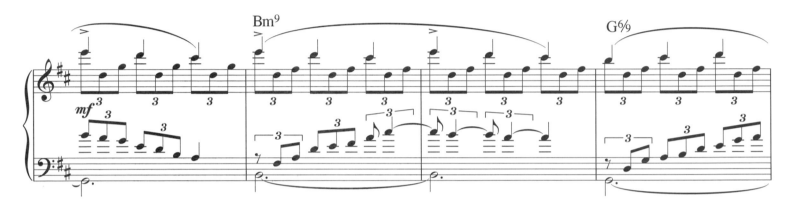

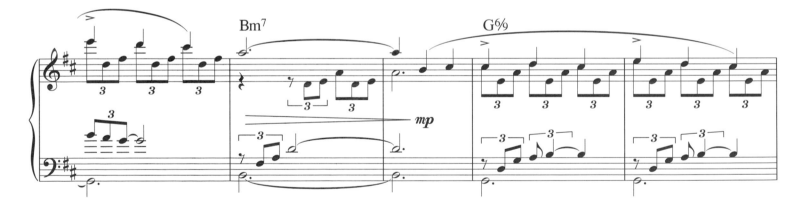

poco rall. _ _ _ _ _ _ _ _ _ _ _ A Tempo Primo

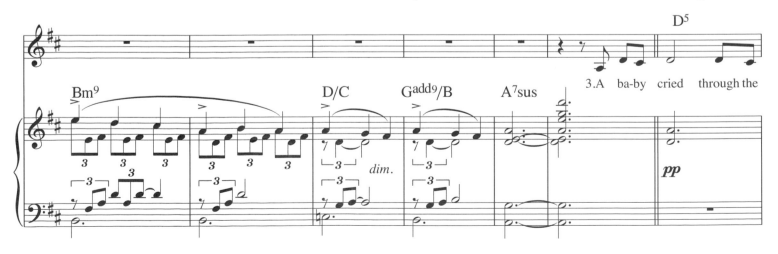

3.A ba-by cried through the

A Mother's Prayer

Words and Music by
Keith Getty, Kristyn Getty
and Fionán de Barra
Piano Arranged by Paul Campbell

Dún do shúil, a rún___ mo chroí A-gus gheob-hair fei-rín___ a-ma-rách.
(Close your eyes, oh love of my heart, and you will get___ a gift___ to-mor-row.)

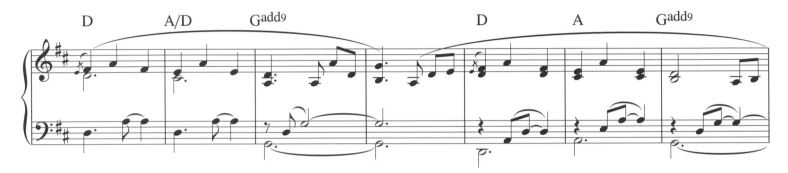

3. You'll tra-vel where my arms won't reach, as the road will rise to
May my mis-takes not hin-der you, but His grace re-main and

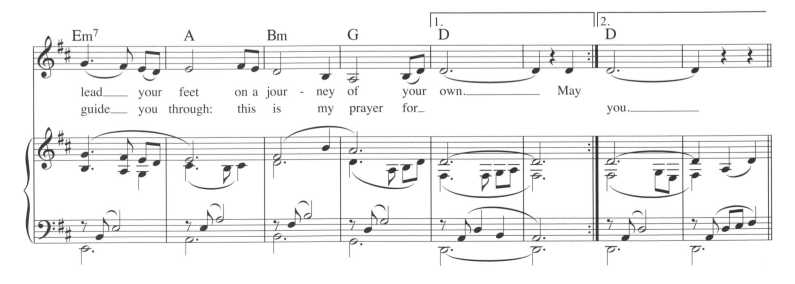

lead___ your feet on a jour-ney of your own.___ May
guide___ you through: this is my prayer for_ you.___

Refrain

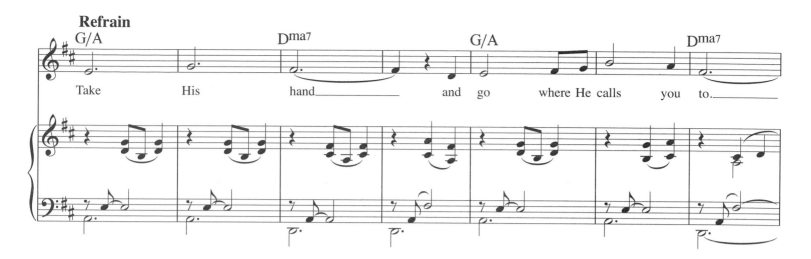

Take His hand_____ and go where He calls you to._____

__ And what-ev-er comes,_____ seek Him with all_____ your_ heart: This will be my

prayer for_ you._____ (Hum)_____ Fath-er,

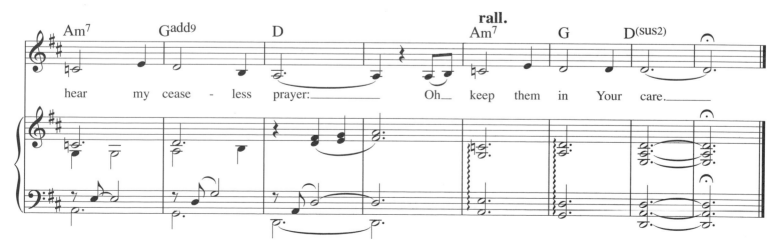

hear my cease - less prayer:_____ Oh_ keep them in Your care._____

Silent Night

Music and Words by Franz Gruber
Arranged by Keith Getty

Thou Who Wast Rich Beyond All Splendor

French Traditional Carol
Words by Frank Houghton
Arranged by Paul Campbell

Deck the Halls

Traditional Welsh Carol
Arranged by Peter Wahlers
and Fionán de Barra

Lively Folk Dance (♩ = 184)

14

la.
la.
la.

Fine

Bethlehem Night

Words and Music by
Keith Getty and Kristyn Getty

1. Peace on earth is the pro-mise on that Beth - le - hem night, As a
2. While the na - tions are ra - ging on that Beth - le - hem night, From this
3. Joy a - wa - kens with - in us on that Beth - le - hem night For this

veil falls from hea - ven to grant us the sight Of a
child in a man - ger there dawns a great Light Where the
child is our Sav - ior, our peace and our life. The for -

Child with our like - ness,___ though pure and di - vine; Of a
earth has been bro - ken___ He comes to make whole, For His
gi - ven find free - dom___ to walk in His grace, And to

King born to save us, From the chains of our pride Of a
mer - cy has spo - ken for the sin - ner's soul, For His
share with each oth - er our Re - deem - er's em - brace, And to

King born to save us from the chains of our pride.
mer - cy has spo - ken for the sin - ner's soul.
share with each oth - er our Re - deem - er's em -

2. While the brace.
3. Joy a -

For To Us a Child Is Born

Words and Music by
Keith Getty and Kristyn Getty

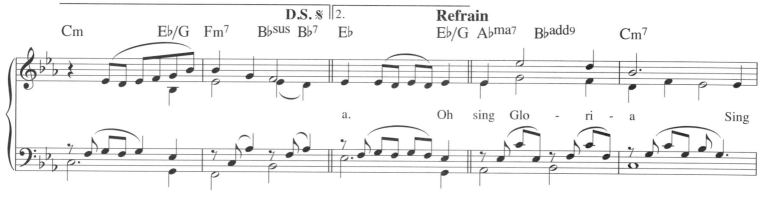

19

O Hear the Bells on Christmas Day

Music: Traditional
Lyrics by Kristyn Getty

1. O hear the bells on Christ-mas day, on Christ-mas day, on Christ-mas day. O hear the bells on Christ-mas day ring
2. We hear the prayers for peace and love, for peace and love, for peace and love. We hear the prayers for peace and love ring
3. We hear the news the an - gels sing, the an - gels sing, the an - gels sing; we hear the news the an - gels sing still

out a - cross the ci - ty. O hear the chil - dren sing with joy, they sing with joy, they
out a - cross the ci - ty. We hear the cry, "Good - will to all!" "Good - will to all!" "Good-
ring a - cross the ci - ty. We hear the news the an - gels sing, the an - gels sing, the

sing with joy. Oh hear the chil - dren sing with joy on Christ - mas Day in the ci - ty.
will to all!" We hear the cry, "Good - will to all!" on Christ - mas Day in the ci - ty.
an - gels sing; we hear the news the an - gels sing still ring a - cross the ci - ty.

Refrain

All those who hear, oh hear Good news of great joy! All those who hear, oh hear Our

Sav- ior is born in Da - vid's ci - ty.

Fine

2. We
3. We

Noël, Noël

Words and Music by
Keith Getty and Kristyn Getty

No - ël, no - ël, oh sing no - ël, join the song of the hea-ven-ly host.

No - ël, no - ël, oh sing no - ël, "Christ is born!" sings the hea-ven-ly host.

1. Hea - ven breaks through the___ skies of Beth-le - hem, "Good news of great joy:___ Christ is born!"
2. Shep - herds re - joice in___ fields of Beth-le - hem; our Sav - ior has come:___ Christ is born!
3. Peo - ple on earth hear___ news of Beth-le - hem; Peace and hope to you:___ Christ is born!

Jesus, Tender Shepherd, Hear Me

Words by Mary Lundy Duncan
Additional Words by Keith Getty, Kristyn Getty
Music by Keith Getty and Kristyn Getty

bless Thy___ lit - tle lamb to night.

Glorious Light!

Words and Music by
Keith Getty. Kristyn Getty
and Ian Hannah

With Energy

1. Glo - ri - ous light! See the dawn of sal - va - tion.
2. Long has the world fought the song of the an - gels;
3. There is a day all crea - a - tion has longed for;

An - gels in white fill the skies with their won - drous
Heav - en - ly mus - ic is drowned by a warr - ing
When all of time has been spent and the Lord re -

song; a - wak - en - ing earth with news of His
world; Yet hope burns a light, that shatt - ers the
turns. His song we'll re - peat, as hea - ven com -

birth. Join the hymn of the high - est heav - ens.
night; turn your heart to the call of glo - ry.
pletes pro - mised peace that will fill the nat - ions.

Refrain

Glo - ry to God in_ the high - est! Peace_ to men on

earth. Come and a - dore Him with won - der;

Christ_ Lord of hea - ven_ and earth.

Jesus, Your Name

Words and Music by
Keith and Kristyn Getty
and Ian Hannah

Simple & Powerful (♩ = 116)

1. Je - sus, Your name, Prince of Peace; Qui - ets my soul, trea - sures the least. In per - fect rest You will keep all whose hope is in You. Je - sus, Your name can si - lence the storms; the striv - ings that trou - ble our world.

2. Je - sus, Your name, Coun - sel - lor; Won - der - ful Way, Life's Com - for - ter. Spi - rit of Truth de - fend - ing me, though in me was the blame. Je - sus, Your name has stood in my place and freed me from hope - less shame;

3. Je - sus, Your name, Migh - ty God; All Pow'r - ful One, rul - ing in love. There is a King up - on the throne earth can - not o - ver-throw. Je - sus, Your name great ban - ner of hope; Stead - ies the knees of the weak.

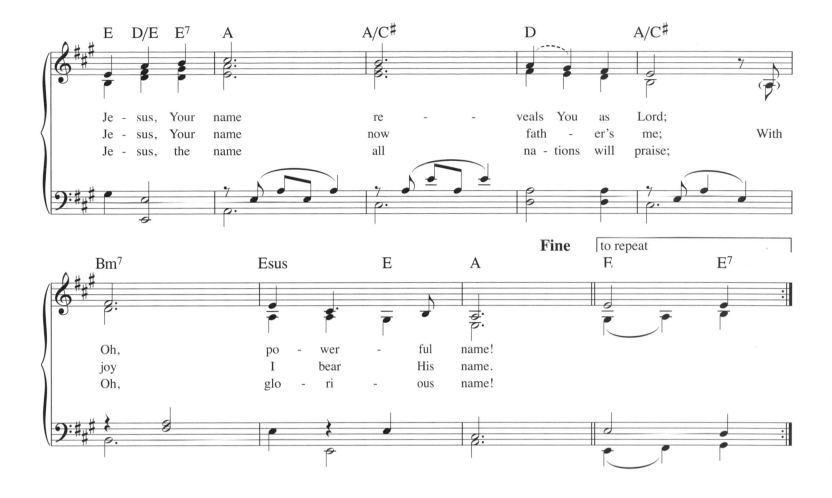

Je - sus, Your name re - - veals You as Lord;
Je - sus, Your name now fath - er's me; With
Je - sus, the name all na - tions will praise;

Oh, po - wer - ful name!
joy I bear His name.
Oh, glo - ri - ous name!

Fine | to repeat

Joy to the World

Lyrics by Isaac Watts
Melody by Lowell Mason
(with themes from George Frideric Handel)
Arranged by Keith Getty and Fionan de Barra

Charlotte's Giggles
(opening reel)

Music by Keith Getty
and Fionán de Barra

Miss Eliza's Reel
(closing reel)

Music by Keith Getty
and Fionán de Barra

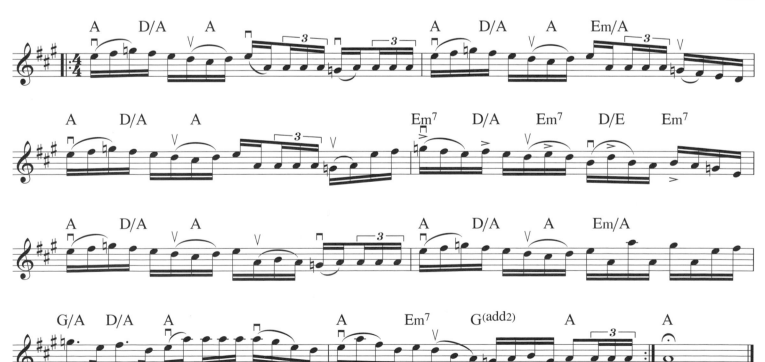

Go, Tell It on the Mountain

Traditional, Arranged by Keith Getty,
Fionán de Barra, Ross Holmes and Zach White

Arkansas Traveler
(opening reel)

Traditional, Arranged by Keith Getty,
Fionán de Barra, Ross Holmes and Zach White

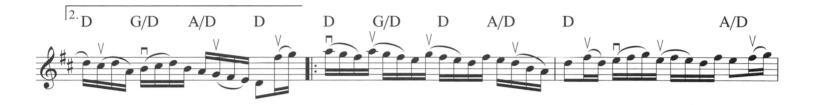

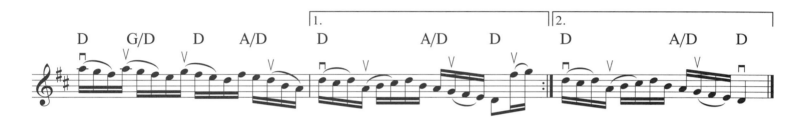

Toss the Feathers
(closing reel)

Traditional, Arranged by Keith Getty,
Fionán de Barra, Ross Holmes and Zach White

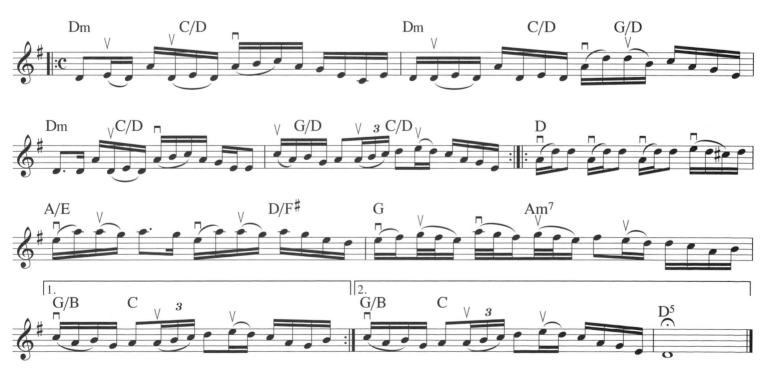

JOY – An Irish Christmas, Vol. 2: The Reels and Jigs

Christmas Eve Reel
(Featured in Sleigh Ride)

Traditional
Arranged by Jeff Taylor

The Silver Spire Reel
(Featured in Deck the Halls)

Traditional
Arranged by Fionán de Barra

Wassailing Jig
(Featured in Here We Come A-Wassailing)

Music by Keith Getty
and Fionán de Barra

Bethlehem Traveler's Reel
(Featured in Ding, Dong, Merrily on High)

Music by Keith Getty
and Ross Holmes

The Voice and Chime
(Featured in O Hear the Bells on Christmas Day)

Music by Keith Getty
and Fionán de Barra

The following two tunes *'Crossing the Briney'* and *'Christmas Ceili'*
(also known as *'Goin' to the Ceili'*) were featured in 2014 on our Joy – An Irish Christmas Tour
and are written by bluegrass legend, Ricky Skaggs. Both songs are featured
on the album *'Instrumentals'* by Ricky Skaggs and Kentucky Thunder.

Crossing the Briney

Music by Ricky Skaggs

Christmas Ceili (Goin' to the Ceili)

Music by Ricky Skaggs

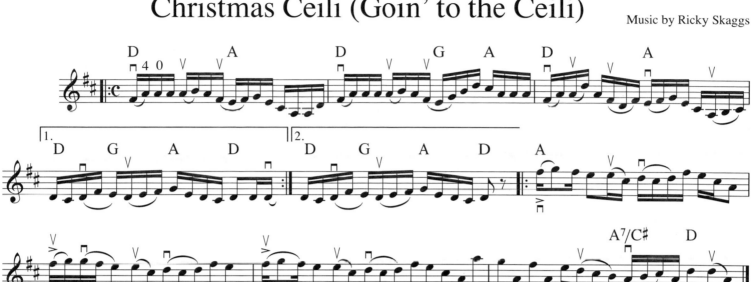

BOOKINGS / SONGBOOKS / TRACKS

For touring information contact: joni@gettymusic.com

Choral versions and orchestrations available at gettymusic.com